# WHERE ARE YOU?

*Returning to His Presence*

## DEBRA YARDE

Where Are You?
Returning to His Presence
Copyright © 2021 Debra Yarde
Cover Design: C Marcel Wiggins

*Rekindled Flame* an imprint of MIGMIR All rights reserved. No part of this publication may be reproduced, distributed or transmitted in any form or by any means, without prior written permission. Unless otherwise identified, scripture quotations are from the King James Version of the Bible.

Published by
MIGMIR Company USA, LLC
P.O. Box 291354
Port Orange, FL 32129

www.migmir.us
For Worldwide Distribution
Printed in the U.S.A.

ISBN: 9781952253119
Library of Congress Control Number: 2021924313

# CONTENTS

Dedication .................................................................. 4

Introduction ............................................................... 5

Chapter One: The light ............................................. 7

Chapter Two: Made in His image ........................... 17

Chapter Three: Wow moment ................................. 31

Chapter Four: Whose voice are you listening to? ... 41

Chapter Five: Why are you hiding? ........................ 55

Chapter Six: The renewed mind .............................. 65

Chapter Seven: It's time to return ........................... 75

Affirmations and prayers .......................................... 79

Debra's Story ............................................................. 83

Verses to help you everyday ..................................... 89

# Dedication

First, giving all honor to my Lord and Savior Jesus Christ. He makes all things possible. I thank Him for every detail of this book.

I also want to dedicate this book to the late, Pastor James Strother (Dad) and Evangelist Shirley Strother (Mom). I love you. I am so grateful for the two of you.

To all four of my children: Cornell, Rafeal, Lakeisha, and Jessica, this book is also dedicated to you.

# Introduction

During a time of seeking God, He gave me this title. Where are You? Returning to the presence of God. I believe that was the question He was asking me. We can get so bombarded with the cares of this world that we forget about our God. We put so many things in front and before Him. We forget He is the Supreme God. He is Ruler over it all. So, when the Lord spoke to me about this book, we had just entered the worst pandemic that hit our nation. Covid 19! So many people lost loved ones. Businesses were closed. Churches were shut down. Nevertheless, what was the most important thing for all of us who believe? Getting back in the presence of God. Returning to a God that we had lost fellowship with. A God that yearned for His people to praise and worship Him.

Like Adam and Eve, they actively hid themselves from His presence acknowledging that their intimate fellowship was broken. Well, we thank God for being the God who restores. He wants to restore us back to the original intent, so that we can once and for all be in His perfect will. It is going to take us really renewing our minds. When we make Him first, we can experience the overflow. God wants to bless us. He wants us to live the abundant life. Where are You? That is the question. Where do you want to be?

# CHAPTER ONE
# THE LIGHT

In the midst of a dark world, light came into being. This light shined on so many things. It allowed us to see and experience the most beautiful things around us. As the light shined bright, it brought about laughter. It brought joy; the light rendered peace. God created light by simply speaking it into existence. God has sovereign dominion over His creation.

Let's review an old science lesson:

Earth has been bathed with light from the sun; it is our most important source of energy. Sunlight warms us. It affects the weather. It allows plants to manufacture oxygen—and our food from carbon dioxide and water. The earth passed through a day and night cycle in reference to this light... *"and God saw the light that it was good."* Light is forever vital to the earth.

According to an article by Technical Consumer Products, Inc. (TCP), a question was asked. "How does light really affect our lives?" The article states, *"Light creates more than just visual effects (image, shape, intensity, perception, contrast, etc.); it also has biological and psychological effects that can impact the health and wellbeing of humans. When light biologically impacts us, it can improve or disrupt our sleep, cognition and overall wellbeing. It can improve mood and stabilize our circadian rhythms, helping us get a better and deeper nights sleep. Psychologically, light can decrease depression scores and even increase cognitive performance such as reaction time and activation."* [1]

# CHAPTER ONE: THE LIGHT

When I am near God's light, I feel joy. I am at ease. There is always a peace! I can remember the elation I first experienced coming into His light. It is always near. He is always there.

You may be wondering why I am talking about "light" when the title of this book is "Where are You? Returning to the Presence of God." Well, God has everything to do with everything. So, the light that we need to experience comes from Him. His life is the light that defines our lives. In God's life man can discover the "light of life," and find true relationship.

> *"When I am near God's light, I feel joy. I am at ease. There is always a peace!"*

As I was sitting in my living room December of 2019, I heard the Lord say so plain to me. "I want you to write your next book and the title will be 'Where are You?'" This title was so fitting as to what we were going to experience throughout the pandemic era with everchanging news, politics, and health information. Not just me, but all believers. Where are You? Where have you been? What have you been doing? These are some of the things that were dropped into my spirit as I was putting together my thoughts concerning this title. God does everything well.

*"And were beyond measure astonished, saying, He hath done all things well." Mark 7:37*

    He will use who He wants when He wants to do His bidding. Consequently, this book hit home. It has made me take a spiritual inventory of my life. When He asked the question Where are You? I answered Him. I am here God. I thought I was where I needed to be. Nevertheless, He is requiring MORE! As I will be posing the question all throughout this book. I want you to take a spiritual inventory of your own life. Asking yourself the same question. "Where are You?"
Are you where you want to be?
Are you concerned about where you are?
Do you care?
Does it matter?

    Let us take off the masks and be real. We have to be real with the Lord. Yes, the real deal. Yes! He knows everything there is to know about us. We can be in denial. We do not want to face the reality of the truth. Therefore, we continue living a lie while knowing that we have missed the mark. We have made people idols. We have put other things before Him. We have broken fellowship. Child of God, God wants us back! He wants us back to the original intent. He wants us to return to His presence. We need God like never before and He knows that.

We live in a world where you hear people say "microwave society." According to the Urban Dictionary, the meaning of "microwave society" is the mindset of wanting (and nearly getting) everything "right now."[2] Technology has made gathering or sending information extremely fast and we've begun to think that everything in life should be available on demand.

> *"We need God like never before and He knows that."*

What does God think?
We will continue to go deeper in the next chapter.
Where are You?

# WHERE ARE YOU?

# CHAPTER ONE: THE LIGHT

# WHERE ARE YOU?

# CHAPTER ONE: THE LIGHT

# WHERE ARE YOU?

# CHAPTER TWO
# MADE IN HIS IMAGE

What a Mighty God we serve. Yes, a God who knew everything we were going to need. A God who took the time to design us, make us, shape us, and mold us into who's image? His! We are made in His image. The Bible describes the origin of the genders as a creative act of God. Mankind will never be able to understand our God and His plan.

His plan is for us to be in continual fellowship with Him. As we stay in constant communion, we will be fruitful—we will multifply. The plan of God is to increase us. As a result, we will produce a quality life.

*"The thief cometh not, but for to steal, and to kill, and to destroy: I am come that they might have life, and that they might have it more abundantly." John 10:10*

Our abundant living was made possible through the death, burial, and resurrection of Jesus Christ, our Lord.
Where are You?

So, when you look at yourself as being fashioned and shaped by God, you should rejoice. Your life was certainly and undeniably by design. So yes, He designed the greatest species on earth. Everything that God made is good. When you look at yourself through the eyes of God, you should not see a failure. You will then understand and realize that your life has meaning. When I finally realized who I was in Christ "fearfully and wonderfully made," I stopped looking at myself as a mistake, mess, or failure. I no longer viewed who I was through the lens of my past; I am created in His image. The way He sees us far greater than we could ever imagine.

## CHAPTER TWO: MADE IN HIS IMAGE

*"I will praise thee; for I am fearfully and wonderfully made: marvellous are thy works; and that my soul knoweth right well."*
Psalms 139:14

Let's take a look back to the garden at the first family, Adam and Eve. They were created with a purpose. Mankind was given a mandate. He gave us an order to subdue and take dominion over it all. There was order and peace in His presence.

*"And God said, Let us make man in our image, after our likeness: and let them have dominion over the fish of the sea, and over the fowl of the air, and over the cattle, and over all the earth, and over every creeping thing that creepeth upon the earth."*
Genesis 1:26

Today, if we look at the crisis in the world, we see our greed, our selfishness, and our carelessness. Let us return to His will—His way. Only then, can we experience the peace and purpose of His plan for us. When we see ourselves in our original image, the evil in this world loses its power over us.

Adam did not look like God in the sense of God having flesh and blood. According to John 4:24, "God is a Spirit" and therefore exists without a body. However, Adam's body did mirror the life of God. It was created in perfect health and was not subject to death.

*"God is a Spirit: and they that worship him must worship him in spirit and in truth." John 4:24*

*"For [d]by Him all things were created in heaven and on earth, [things] visible and invisible, whether thrones or dominions or rulers or authorities; all things were created and exist through Him [that is, by His activity] and for Him. And He Himself existed and is before all things, and in Him all things hold together. [His is the controlling, cohesive force of the universe. Colossians 1:16-17 (AMP)*

Humanity was created in righteousness and perfect innocence. Again, God called us "good." No matter what we have done, He loves us. He sees us as His children that He created and sustains. When I look at the biblical definition of good: It says we are pure, holy, and righteous. That's how He sees us. The Bible states "Love has been perfected among us in this that we may have boldness in the day of judgment because as He is so are we in this world." What a wonderful thing to be made in His image.

God made us to be in fellowship with Him. When we are in fellowship His heart is overjoyed. We were created for Worship with the King. All Glory and Honor rightfully belongs to God. He created us so that we would glorify Him. Therefore, it is your duty to live for God's Glory. Where are you?

A part of being made in God's image is that Adam had the capacity to make free choices. Although they were given a righteous nature, Adam and Eve made an evil choice to rebel against their Creator. So what about us? The Bible says we all have sinned and fallen short. We all have been deceived by the devil himself. That's why God sent His only Son into the world to redeem us back to the original intent. God wants us to be in His presence so He can show us things through the power of the Holy Spirit.

When God redeems an individual, He begins to restore their original image, creating a "new self," created to be like God in true righteousness and holiness. God wants us to immerse ourselves into this God-shaped new person from above. You are created in the image and likeness of God. This is what true righteousness and holiness is all about. This is good news! Praise the Lord, we shout Glory.

A relationship with God is of vital importance so you can mirror your King. Glory! You must understand and know your identity in Christ. You must know who you are. God wants you to know the price He paid for you through Christ. Through Christ, you are made in the image of God. Accept your reality. It's time to be real. Will the real you please stand up. It is time to take your rightful place. Get in alignment with our Lord and Savior. Align yourself with the truth of who you are. Made in His image and His likeness. It is time to replace the lie with the truth. The enemy lied to Adam and Eve. He also lies to us. However, enough is enough! It's time to come out of darkness and into the light. It is time to stand and see yourself as a "whosoever." *For God so loved the world that He gave His only begotten Son. That whosoever believeth in Him should not perish but have everlasting life.*

The Bible says, *"God is not a man that He should lie, neither the son of man that He should repent. Hath He said, and shall He not do it? Or hath He spoken, and shall He not make it good."* Well you have been made good. Glory!

## CHAPTER TWO: MADE IN HIS IMAGE

I just get excited to understand and know that everything God's hand touched was made good. Man has touched things and made it bad through the devil. But you blessed one are the real deal. We are the real deal, because of our Redeemer. His love for us...fashioned us in the image of Himself. His love is so amazing. His love is so incredible. It is up to you to accept it, believe it, and receive it.

A word of encouragement: This book has helped me return to loving a God who never stopped loving me. He has always loved me. As I read scriptures, I allowed them to come alive in me. The Lord wants us to come alive in Him. Then, we really can live, and not just exist. When we think about our lives, we discover that God loved us so much—even when we were doing wrong. Adam and Eve did wrong but, He went looking for them to restore them back to the original intent. God loves you! He has made you a new creation.

*"Therefore if any man be in Christ, he is a new creature: old things are passed away; behold, all things are become new."*
*II Corinthians 5:17*

Let us walk in that newness to be what He has intended for us to be.

When I look at my life, I just have to be transparent and say, I did not mirror God. I made some mistakes. My life did not reflect the One who said I was made in His image and in His likeness—it was more of darkness, shame, and guilt. The enemy wanted me to stay in a defeated state. He didn't want me to realize who I was in Christ. The thought of being like God in His image was nowhere in my mind. Everyone has sinned. I really don't understand why we can't just be who God has called us to be. It is time for us to stop beating each other up with the negativity, especially regarding the past. The church folk, (some I should say) can be so hard on one another instead of just letting it go. The Bible says we are free from condemnation. The debt has been canceled; God has forgiven us. Nevertheless, so many people have left the church for the reason of being judged by others for the things they've done. Who are we to cast a stone? We must take a look in the mirror at our own lives and show love. I know first hand what it's like to be "ousted." Yes, to be made to feel as though you just don't belong. It hurts.

> *"The enemy wanted me to stay in a defeated state. He didn't want me to realize who I was in Christ."*

## CHAPTER TWO: MADE IN HIS IMAGE

God put me right back into a place of believing and trusting in Him and myself; thank God He lifted me. I can make it. I must make it, because of Who I belong to.

I know the Lord is leading me to deal with the phrase "Church Hurt." When folk come for you, at the time it does hurt. You will feel a sense of betrayal. However, we must get over it and move on. So many anointed and appointed people are sitting at home right now. Many, because of an offense they have allowed the enemy to win. Some stopped fellowshipping and coming to church. Now, all they do is work. They are working for themselves and not for kingdom. This mindset is quite selfish; we must deal with it. Your hurt and your pain was taken to the cross. We should no longer continue to make excuses about why we don't serve the Lord because of people. Stop sitting and singing "somebody did me wrong." God forgive us. God forgive me. Yes, I was one of those people. But, thank God for Jesus. I asked God to forgive me, and to forgive the one who offended me. Now, I am free to move into the things of God. I wanted to stay mad and use excuses. That thinking was getting me nowhere but stuck! It's time to be renewed. It's time to be refreshed. Get back in His presence and encounter all that He has for you. He has a plan for you.

*"For I know the thoughts that I think toward you, saith the Lord, thoughts of peace, and not of evil, to give you an expected end." Jeremiah 29:11*

We cannot afford to allow anything or anybody to take us out of the will of the Father. Remember, you are made in His image.

# CHAPTER TWO: MADE IN HIS IMAGE

# WHERE ARE YOU?

## CHAPTER TWO: MADE IN HIS IMAGE

## WHERE ARE YOU?

# CHAPTER THREE
# WOW MOMENT

I am at a loss for words. I do not know where to begin. I was writing this book, "Where are you? Returning to the Presence of God." I was stuck and could not understand why the book was not flowing. Was I experiencing writer's block? God is faithful and my trust is in Him.
Even when we think we can't, He will always make a way.

On May 26, 2021, I went to visit my father in the hospital. When I got to his room, he was not there. The nurse told me he went for a procedure. Soon after he returned, he was sleeping. I saw his eyes open and he noticed that I was there. He started perking up when he looked at me.

I asked, "How are you?"

He softly said, "ok."

I noticed he was not looking like himself. My father had been looking weak for some time. I got up, went over to him, and rubbed him on his head and told him I loved him. He said he loved me too. That was one thing about my daddy, he would always tell us he loved us.

In August of 2020, we had a scare with him. He basically died for 51 seconds. The Lord allowed him to come back to us for 10 months. So in the room that day, May 26, 2021, I could tell Dad was going home. We talked for a little while and I kissed him and said a prayer. Dad was a man of few words. I knew it was hard for him to breathe, even though he was being tough and didn't want me to know. If there was one thing you could get him to talk about, it would be the Bible and the Lord. You could not shut him up. So, I left the hospital and went home. That was the last time I saw him. May 28, 2021 at 5:30a.m. he was gone. It really was a shock to us. We did not get a chance to say goodbye. The first man on earth to tell me he loved me was gone. There is nothing like a father's love. He knows what to say, and when to say it. I am so grateful and thankful for the 58 years I got to spend with my dad. What makes this so grand, is that he introduced me to someone who would always be with me—my Lord and Savior Jesus Christ. So, the first Father's Day without him, what can I say? He is back in the presence of God.

*"We are confident, I say, and willing rather to be absent from the body, and to be present with the Lord."*
*II Corinthians 5:8*

What a "Wow" Moment. My Dad is now present with the Lord. That's reassuring! I am convinced (without a shadow of a doubt) that he is at peace. For those who have ever lost a loved one who died in Christ, this is good news. This was the first time in over five years we had a death in our family. Our grandmother had died. She was my dad's mom. Her death took a big toll on him. After that, it just seemed he was so lost, although trying to keep it together. We knew her dying was a very emotional strain on him. I can remember when coming to him and asking him for something, it would not always be, "Yes daughter you can have this." Sometimes, he would say, "Wait." Well, I didn't want to wait. I wanted it when I wanted it with no questions. The loving dad he was, he would look up at me and just smile and say, "Wait." So, of course I didn't have a choice. Just like God, a loving father knows what is best for us. We must always trust the process. Even in the wait, we should be maturing, growing, and learning what's the best thing for us. God knows He has the blueprint for us all. So, why not get back in His presence and receive instructions from Him?

So many people have lost loved ones due to Covid and other things. With death, you are never really prepared for the loss. We had no idea our dad was going to die so fast and leave us. So, how am I dealing with it? How am I getting through it? It's all because of Jesus. Sometimes, I start thinking about my dad and the way he loved and always cared for me. No matter if I was wrong, he always came to my defense. I miss him so much.

# CHAPTER THREE: WOW MOMENT

I am the oldest daughter, the first born, so I did get special treatment. I really realize all of the sacrifices he made for me down through the years. Unfortunately, I took a lot of things for granted, thinking he would always be here for us. We needed him, but God needed him more. I will always love the second man in my life, God is the first. They say I look just like him. That I mirror the reflection of my earthly dad. He is missed, and I know he would want me to continue on the battlefield for my Lord. Dad, I love you with all my heart. You loved me just like God would love me. Taking care of us, working hard for us, and teaching us to love one another. I miss your smile and laughter. I miss you fussing at me because I didn't add enough salt in your food. It's all good.

It was January, the first Sunday of 2020, when he walked in the church and said, "I am handing the church over to Debra." We all were shocked. I am proud he left a legacy. Dad, you are not here in the flesh anymore. We know you are resting with God. Son bear, we love you.

— *Your daughter, Debra*

So, when you ask me how I am doing? I tell you, it is well with my soul.

# CHAPTER THREE: WOW MOMENT

## WHERE ARE YOU?

# CHAPTER THREE: WOW MOMENT

# WHERE ARE YOU?

# CHAPTER FOUR
# WHOSE VOICE ARE YOU LISTENING TO?

My earthly father fought so hard to get me back on track. Why? I was out of order and not in correct alignment with God. He knew as a father, his job was to save his daughter. He did just that. He came after me, him and my mom and moved everything that was blocking them from getting to me.

It didn't matter who or what it was. God used them to get me back where I needed to be because I was lost. Like Eve, when the serpent tempted her to do wrong, she failed. She did not listen to the instructions of God. Some of us have listened to wrong voices. When I was reading the portion of scripture (in Genesis) when the devil tempted Eve, it was so real. This devil will come at you swiftly. If you are not prayed up, you will mess up.

*"Now the serpent was more subtle than any beast of the field which the LORD God had made. And he said unto the woman, Yea, hath God said, Ye shall not eat of every tree of the garden? And the woman said unto the serpent, we may eat of the fruit of the trees of the garden: But of the fruit of the tree which is in the midst of the garden, God hath said, Ye shall not eat of it, neither shall ye touch it, lest ye die. And the serpent said unto the woman, Ye shall not surely die: For God doth know that in the day ye eat thereof, then your eyes shall be opened, and ye shall be as gods, knowing good and evil. And when the woman saw that the tree was good for food, and that it was pleasant to the eyes, and a tree to be desired to make one wise, she took of the fruit thereof, and did eat, and gave also unto her husband with her; and he did eat."*

*Genesis 3:1-6*

## CHAPTER FOUR: WHOSE VOICE ARE YOU LISTENING TO?

Unlike us Eve downplayed what God really said. God didn't say if you "touch" the fruit, He said if you "eat" the fruit, you will surely die. Surely is a word that means it's definitely going to happen. That is, death upon eating the fruit. They were given their instructions.

Satan said, "You will not surely die." So, let's look at the play on words:
In the King James Version of the bible,
God said, "You will surely die."
Eve said, "Lest ye die."
Satan said, "Again, you will not surely die."
When you look at how satan used the word surely as God did, he knew what God had said to Eve. With his power of persuasion, he tricked her with a lie. The devil had her convinced she was not going to die. He also lied to her and said to her, "For God doth know that in the day ye eat thereof, then your eyes shall be opened, and ye shall be as gods knowing good and evil." When Eve looked at the tree, this was an evaluation process of the mind. The tree was good for food and appealed to the appetite. [The lust of the flesh.] It was pleasant to the eyes. [The lust of the eyes.] The bible clearly states in I John 2:16:

*"For all that is in the world the lust of the flesh and the lust*

*of the eyes, and the pride of life is not the Father, but is of the world."*

Notice how Adam was with her. The Bible says, "She took of the fruit thereof and did eat and gave also unto her husband with her and he did eat." Both of them disobeyed the voice of God and listened to the voice of the enemy. The question is, why would they trade their position with a lie? They did not realize their true position. They were already like God. According to Genesis 2:27, God created man in His image in the image of God...male and female created He them. The bible says, "the serpent was more subtle than any beast of the field which the Lord God had made." The devil was crafty and had discernment.

When we think about our lives, the enemy has tricked and trapped many of us into doing things that were out of the will of the Father. Through our own experiences, we see how he persuaded the first family to sin against God and what He said. This is the whole problem with satan, he wants us to go against what God HAS SAID. Our adversary wants us to listen to his voice, instead of the voice of God. This is why I asked the question, "Whose voice are we listening to?"

## CHAPTER FOUR: WHOSE VOICE ARE YOU LISTENING TO?

I don't know why Eve listened to the devil. What did she think of this serpent speaking to her? Maybe she thought it was a "good angel" speaking to her. Sometimes what seems right, can be so wrong. All I know, is what God said. As we look deeper, we can see that the temptation itself, (or the fall) was man's greatest mistake. But, God can turn your mess up into a blessing. Satan wants to always place doubt on what God has said to His children. When we have made up our minds to serve God, he wants us to second guess ourselves. We must make sure, without a shadow of a doubt, that we obey what He says. For us women, satan came after the weaker vessel. At moments when no one is around he will tempt us. He often uses distractions so that our minds are not focused and we are not watching. Always remember, fear has a voice; faith has a voice. Which one are you listening to? We must allow faith to rise in our hearts. We must believe and trust what God says. The devil, (as we see in Genesis) will place that doubt in you. The devil wants to destroy you. We must stand up as believers, and let the devil know we will stand on what God says. We will hear His voice and obey Him.

> *"But, God can turn your mess up into a blessing."*

*"My sheep hear My voice, and I know them, and they follow*

Me." John 10:27

There are a lot of voices in this world screaming for attention, wanting and needing to be heard. Voices do have significance

*"There are, it may be, so many kinds of voices in the world, and none of them is without signification."*
*I Corinthians 14:10*

Let's go deeper. There is the audible voice of another person that you recognize and know when you hear it. We must understand that the voice of man can give wise counsel, but it should never override the voice of God. We must obey God at all times. He knows what we need when we need it. He sacrificed His Son to die for us. He knows everything before it happens. The Bible says,

*"For we are his workmanship, created in Christ Jesus for good works, which God prepared beforehand, that we should walk in them." Ephesians 2:10*

He is our God. We should obey Him at all times. If He tells you to do something, just do it. Praise the Lord! Just do it. When you obey Him, you will see the blessings flowing in your life. You will see favor come on you like never before. Why, because you are in truth. The voice of satan led Adam and Eve down a road of despair and failure. They committed high treason against God because they listened to a strange voice. Well, don't leave us out. We too have listened to strange voices. We didn't take the time to seek the truth. Satan's voice lies. It misinforms and attempts to lead man away from God into sin.

*"Then was Jesus led up of the Spirit into the wilderness to be tempted of the devil. And when he had fasted forty days and forty nights, he was afterward an hungred. And when the tempter came to him, he said, If thou be the Son of God, command that these stones be made bread. But he answered and said, It is written, Man shall not live by bread alone, but by every word that proceedeth out of the mouth of God. Then the devil taketh him up into the holy city, and setteth him on a pinnacle of the temple, And saith unto him, If thou be the Son of God, cast thyself down: for it is written, He shall give his angels charge concerning thee: and in their hands they shall bear thee up, lest at any time thou dash thy foot against a stone. Jesus said unto him, It is written again, Thou shalt not tempt the Lord thy God. Again, the devil taketh him up into an exceeding high mountain, and sheweth him all the kingdoms of the world, and the glory of them; And saith unto him, All these things will I give thee, if*

*thou wilt fall down and worship me. Then saith Jesus unto him, Get thee hence, Satan: for it is written, Thou shalt worship the Lord thy God, and him only shalt thou serve. Matthew 4:1-10*

> "Wanting to fulfill the lust of the flesh gets us in trouble everytime."

So, he even tried to get our Lord and Savoir in a lie. The Lord knew His purpose. He also knew the counterfeit voice of His adversary. It was not the voice of His Father. Adam and Eve did not follow the plan of God. They listened to the voice of Satan and ate of the forbidden tree. When they realized what they had done, they hid themselves from the Lord. Think about this: Adam and Eve knew the voice of God. They heard Him.

They talked to Him. They had fellowship with Him. So, they knew His voice. But why didn't they know the voice of a stranger? Eve saw the fruit. She liked what she saw. When the serpant spoke, making his presentation, something agreed with her and she wanted more. Always be grateful for what you have. Eve didn't realize that she had it all. She was already made in God's image and in His likeness, she did not need to fall victim to satan's ploy.

*"And when the woman saw that the tree was good for food and*

*that it was pleasant to the eyes and a tree to be desired to make one wise." Genesis 3:6*

We can see the appeal to her appetite. We can also see the lust of the flesh in operation. Wanting to fulfill the lust of the flesh gets us in trouble everytime. Stop feeling the need to listen to all of the "sweet nothings" that the counterfeit tells us. It is sin which separates man from God. God did not remove His presence from man because of sin. Man hid himself from the presence of God. Where are you?

# WHERE ARE YOU?

## CHAPTER FOUR: WHOSE VOICE ARE YOU LISTENING TO?

# WHERE ARE YOU?

## CHAPTER FOUR: WHOSE VOICE ARE YOU LISTENING TO?

# WHERE ARE YOU?

# CHAPTER FIVE
# WHY ARE YOU HIDING?

In the previous chapter we talked about the voice of God. Also, the importance of obeying our Father and not listening to the voice of the devil. When we talk about sin and its results, we must realize the importance of getting back in the presence of God. The broken fellowship needs to be repaired. We need to be in relationship with Him. I know I need to be in constant fellowship with my God. He is the most important person on this Earth. We need Him.

He is our Savior, our Lord, and our King. He is our Healer. He is our Deliverer. Why do we hide from Him when we mess up? He knows when we have messed up. Its okay if you have made some mistakes. I know I have. I am thankful that God is not holding it against me. He loves me. He wants me in His presence. Even when I mess up. When you don't feel Him, don't panic. We can't escape Him. Why would we want to escape or avoid Him? Our shame or guilt doesnt need to be hid from Him. Why? He already knows. He knows every single hair strand on your head. We can be restored and renewed. Why run away when we should be running to Him? Adam and Eve knew they had messed up, so they hid from God.

*"And the eyes of them both were opened and they knew they were naked and they sew fig leaves together and made themselves aprons." Genesis 3:7*

    In Genesis Chapter 2:25 it reads *"And they were both naked the man and his wife and were not ashamed."* Lets look at this. Their outward nakedness was a sign of integrity. They lived and moved without guilt nor shame, no fear of exploitation or threat. Their identity was in what God said. "Made in His image and likeness." Adam even said this woman is now "bone of my bone flesh of my flesh." They were so excited to be one.

*"The thief cometh not, but for to steal, and to kill, and to destroy: I am come that they might have life, and that they might have it more abundantly." John 10:10*

We know the thief comes to steal, kill, and destroy. Yes, you may see the truth. You might know the truth of who you are. However, it's his job to deceive. He wants to get you off course away from God's plan.

We know for ourselves that we can be living on top of the world one minute—one wrong decision can have us in a place of regret. When Adam and Eve sinned, the sense of guilt was immediate. They went from knowing who they were "naked and unashamed," [unapologeticly] to "naked and ashamed." Just by listening to the wrong voice, everything immediately changed. Help us God! Forgive us God!

We are constantly reminded of what satan did to the first family. They walked and talked with God. They knew His voice but still got off track. We have to be better than that. We have to return back to the presence so we can know what He is saying to us. He wants to be in fellowship with His children. Yes, we all have sinned. God is not holding that against us. He wants us to repent and turn back to Him. Not to stay in guilt and shame.

He knew we were going to mess up. That's why He sent Jesus to save us from ourselves. He knew like Adam and Eve, we were going to be tempted and fail. But to God be all the Glory there is no failure in God.

*"There is therefore now no condemnation to them which are in Christ Jesus, who walk not after the flesh, but after the Spirit" Romans 8:1*

*"This I say then, Walk in the Spirit, and ye shall not fulfil the lust of the flesh." Galatians 5:16*

Hiding from God is not the answer. We have to walk in the Spirit.

*"Be sober, be vigilant; because your adversary the devil, as a roaring lion, walketh about, seeking whom he may devour:" I Peter 3:8*

He wants to devour you. He wants to take you out.

When we hide from God, we are looking at the carnal nature. We cannot afford to operate with a carnal nature, which causes selfish motives, and doing things that will cause you to sin. Without God, your life has no purpose and no meaning. You are just existing; you're not living. God wants us to live. He wants us to know who we are in Christ.

John 15:5 says,

*"I am the vine, ye are the branches: He that abideth in me, and I in him, the same bringeth forth much fruit: for without me ye can do nothing."*

I was in my backyard. I noticed there was a branch that was hanging on the tree. It had withered and turned all brown. It was still attached to the tree, but it was broken in two. It could no longer get the proper nourishments to keep it alive. Thank God for Jesus. He will always be the source of our supply. No matter if we hide from Him when we mess up. Adam and Eve came to know their intimate fellowship with God had been broken. He called out for them saying, "Adam Where are thou?" Where are you? God always seeks man out. He knew what happened. God felt the broken fellowship as well. He came asking a question, not making accusation. Where are you? There is nothing that you will do that will keep Him from seeking you out. He loves you unconditionally. You have to let His love be your reality. That's why He sent Jesus. We must get back where God can find us well with Him—in His will. Loving on Him. We live in a world with so much uncertainty. It is very important that we get back to prayer, back to the altar, and back to being in the presence of our God.

# CHAPTER FIVE: WHY ARE YOU HIDING?

# WHERE ARE YOU?

# CHAPTER FIVE: WHY ARE YOU HIDING?

# WHERE ARE YOU?

# CHAPTER SIX
# THE RENEWED MIND

Your mind is naturally conformed to the principles of the world around you. The conformity happens because of your basic sin nature. It also manifests through the influence of your society. [God] says, "You are not to conform to the world but to be transformed." The word "transform" means to be changed or into a new image.

The pattern for that image is the Lord Jesus Christ:

*"But we all, with open face, beholding as in a glass the glory of the Lord, are changed into the same image from glory to glory, even as by the Spirit of the Lord." (II Corinthians 3:18)*

According to Romans 12:2, transformation comes through renewing your mind. This means you must get rid of worldly standards and principles and conform to the principles revealed in God's written Word. Your mind is transformed as you develop the mind of Christ:

*"Let this mind be in you which was also in Christ Jesus." Philippians 2:5*

The word "let" indicates that you have to make a choice in order to have the mind of Christ. You must permit the transformation of the mind to happen. You have a responsibility in doing this. As you can see, Adam and Eve did not allow what God said to matter. They followed the voice of someone else. In order for us to be obedient to God, we have to have a renewed mind. Our minds must be made up to seek our God and to follow Him.

## CHAPTER SIX: THE RENEWED MIND

*"But seek ye first the kingdom of God, and his righteousness; and all these things shall be added unto you."* Matthew 6:33

In the Garden Adam and Eve had everything they could possibly imagine.

*"But of the tree of the knowledge of good and evil, thou shalt not eat of it, for in the day that thou eatest therefore thou shalt surely die,"* Genesis 2:1

God gave them instruction. Does what He says really matter? Are the things He says to us important? Yes, everything He says to us matters. God wants us to live consistent with who we really are inspired by His loving kindness. The Bible states in the TPT translation, "Stop imitating the ideals and opinions of the culture around you. But be inwardly transformed by the Holy Spirit through a total reformation of how you think. This will empower to discern God's will as you live a beautiful life satisfying and perfect in his eyes." Stop being pulled into the thinking of the world and its compromises.

I was talking to a woman that was so confused about

her life. She was living with a man, going to church and knew she was living wrong. She said, "Debra everybody is doing it." I said just because everybody is doing it doesn't make it right in the eyesight of God. We know that living with a man and not being married is outside of the will of God. But that's the thinking of a carnal mind. Everybody is doing it. Trust me, I had a carnal mind. But the scripture clearly states a carnal mind is against God. Living outside of His will is against Him. He wants us back in right relationship and in right standing with Him. We must learn to live by the Word and obey it. When we live by it we can see the fruit of it.

*"I beseech you therefore, brethren, by the mercies of God, that ye present your bodies a living sacrifice, holy, acceptable unto God, which is your reasonable service. And be not conformed to this world: but be ye transformed by the renewing of your mind, that ye may prove what is that good, and acceptable, and perfect, will of God." Romans 12:1-2*

Let's look at the root of the situation. When we allow sin to take a root in us, it produces bad fruit. Fruit must be cut out of us so we can breathe. If we don't get to the root cause

## CHAPTER SIX: THE RENEWED MIND

of the situation, then we will continue to live a lie. The mind is a terrible thing to waste. The mind is wasted when we have the lies of the devil planted in us. My friend knew she was living wrong. She chose to continue to stay in fornication because everyone else is doing it. I can't judge her. I just want her free. She has to want to be free. She has to want to be in obedience to God. That's all of us. When we decide to make intelligent decisions to live for Christ, and make godly decisions, our lives will never be the same.

> *"When we allow sin to take a root in us, it produces bad fruit."*

It is time to get it right. Jesus is soon to return. If we don't change, if we don't turn back to God, we are going to spend eternity separated from Him. I know I don't want to be seperated from Him. What must we do? We must be born again. We must renew our minds so that we can experience the life He created us to live. David says in Psalm 23,

*"The Lord is my Shepherd I shall not want. He maketh me to lie down in green pastures, He restores my soul."*

Restoration is available for you today. It is accessible. He is waiting for you to return to His presence. I was thinking about the times I stayed away from Him out of ignorance.

*"Finally, brethren, whatsoever things are true, whatsoever things are honest, whatsoever things are just, whatsoever things are pure, whatsoever things are lovely, whatsoever things are of good report; if there be any virtue, and if there be any praise, think on these things." Phillipians 4:8*

When we think on those things that are true, it is the evidence in Christ. Our lives should be showing evidence that Christ is residing in us. When we make up our minds, we are going to live a righteous life because of the likeness of God in us. I have the likeness of God living in me. That's enough to make you scream, shout, and dance. I get so excited when I think about it. He is living in me, and I am one with Him. We must engage our thoughts with throne room realties where we are co-seated together with Christ. Don't be pulled in different directions or worried about a thing. Be saturated in prayer throughout each day, offering your faith filled request before God with overflowing gratitude. We must keep our thoughts continually fixed on all that is authentic, honorable, admirable, beautiful, respectful, pure, holy, merciful, and kind. Having the correct mindset is so important to our mental health. Our mind is a very important part of who we are.

# WHERE ARE YOU?

# CHAPTER SIX: THE RENEWED MIND

# WHERE ARE YOU?

# CHAPTER SEVEN
# IT'S TIME TO RETURN

In the pages of this book we have covered some important things. The most important thing I want you to know is God misses your presence. He wants you back in fellowship with Him; He loves you. The bible states Genesis 3:8 And they heard the voice of the Lord God walking in the garden in the "cool of the day." They hid themselves from the presence of the Lord God amongst the trees. When Adam and Eve hid themselves that let us know that the fellowship was broken.

That was the first result of sin, a sense of shame and fear.

*"The Lord also thundered in the heavens and the Highest gave his voice..." Psalms 18:13a*

Adam and Eve scattered in fear at the voice of God. Yet in that moment, they knew His voice and still allowed the enemy to deceive them. God always seeks out man. He knew Adam and Eve were lost. It proves man's sin and God's grace. Grace, oh Grace, what would we do without Grace? God came asking a question. He comes in love, never condemning us.

I am sitting here getting full because of the love of God and how much He cares for us. A lot of my life was lived with guilt and shame of my past. My past does not define me. Your past does not define you. Jesus' blood covered us. He knew what Adam and Eve had done. This was His creation. One that He looked on and said it was good. We are His greatest creation. That's why it is so important that we let go of the pain and return to the presence of God. In the presence of God we will find rest. We will find Him and again, encounter Him like never before. God does not want us lost. Our position must be saved, sanctified, and filled with the Holy

Ghost. He died for you to carry the title of UNDEFEATED! A WINNER! Yes you are. If you could just believe and receive that. The devil has clouded the minds of those who don't believe. The devil has blinded the eyes so people can't see the truth of the Word. The bible says in Mark 16:16 "He that believed and is baptized shall be saved but he that believed not shall be damned." There is no neutral ground. We are either on the side of Christ or the devil. Jesus said,

"He that is not with Me is against Me, and that gathered not with Me scattereth abroad."

I don't want to be scattered abroad, but only in His presence. S, let's return back to the presence of God. We don't have to hide from Him anymore. He knows everything about us. He knows what we are going to do before we do it. He knows our thoughts. He knows every strain of hair that is on our heads. Why do we hide our faults? God sent Jesus into the world to save us. It's really our choice whether we follow Him. He is knocking on the tables of your heart waiting for you. If you were to die tonight where would you go? To Heaven or to Hell? That's a personal choice. God gave us free will. So you decide. Where are you?

God wants you to know that even though you have sinned, you have not done anything that He would not forgive. That's why this book is being written for you and me to know and understand that we have a purpose and a destiny. In Him, we live and move and have our being. It's because of Christ we can live free. It's because of Christ we can walk with our heads held free from guilt, shame, or fear. Don't let fear stop you from receiving what is rightfully yours. God is waiting—waiting for the return of a people that was created in good works. He is waiting on a people who were with Him before the foundation of the world. Who were given an opportunity to make Him Lord of their lives. God is still waiting. I keep hearing that. God is waiting on you. His love will never fail. His banner over us is love.

He says,

"I am waiting."

# DAILY AFFIRMATIONS

I am born of the incorruptible seed

I am delivered from the power of darkness

I am redeemed from the curse of the law

I am the head and not the tail

I am the elect of God

I am set free

I am strong in the Lord

I am complete in Him

I am alive in Christ

I am free from condemnation

I am free to share in His inheritance

I am overtaken with the blessings

I am the righteousness of God

I am an ambassador for Christ

I am justified completely forgiven and made righteous

My life is hid with Christ in God

I shall overcome because greater is He that is in me than he that is in the world...

I press toward the mark for the prize of the high calling of God

I always triumph in Christ

My life is hid with Christ in God

I know who I am

My Prayer:

*Lord, I return back to You. Forgive me for doubting You. Forgive me from hiding myself from You. I am here. I am Yours. Thank You for giving me the opportunity to return back to You. Thank You for giving me another chance in Jesus' name, Amen.*

# DAILY PRAYERS

### Monday

Father I thank You in the name of Jesus for giving me the strength and the power to be an overcomer. Thank You for accepting me for who I am in Jesus' name, Amen.

### Tuesday

Father help me to know Your voice. Train me to listen to and follow You for the rest of my days. Help me to know when You are speaking to me in Jesus' name, Amen.

### Wednesday

Father please forgive us for holding on to those things of the past. Thank You for washing us and making us new, in Jesus' name, Amen.

### Thursday

Father in the name of Jesus, thank You for making me a confident Kingdom servant. Lord it is in Your power and Your might that You have made me who I am in God. Thank You for sending Your Word and it is what it says I am. In Jesus' name, Amen.

## Friday

Father in the name of Jesus, I thank You for looking beyond my faults and seeing my needs. Thank You Lord in Jesus' name, Amen.

## Saturday

Father in the name of Jesus, thank You for Your everlasting love. Thank You for Your love that reaches to the depth of my soul, and pulls me into purpose. I thank You for loving me. In Jesus' name, Amen.

## Sunday

Father in the name of Jesus, You are a Holy God. I desire to be holy and set apart unto You. Lord help me to live my life in a manner that is pleasing to You. In Jesus' name, Amen.

## Debra's Story

In life we need to be honest and true. I believe when we are, God sees us in a different way. I am here today because of His grace and mercy. I am here today because I surrendered my heart to God. My life was broken and shattered into pieces. I hid from God. I had low self-esteem while looking for love in all the wrong places. I am still wondering sometimes who I am. Life sometimes will deal you a hand that you can't handle. You noticed I said (I) could not handle it. But, God in all His wisdom knows exactly what I needed. I needed to get back in His presence. I am not lost because I can see clearly. No longer blinded by a lie. I am living in the truth of who God made me to be; in His Image and likeness. I am not walking in fear, doubt, and unbelief. I understand and know who I am in Christ.

Life is not easy. When you put your trust in God, and make up in your mind that God is your everything, your life will never be the same. I am a witness. Some days I don't know, but I trust Him. Some days I don't have money, but I trust Him. If you return to God and His presence, your life will be prosperous. He's waiting. No matter what you have done, He is waiting. God wants us to live the life He desires. He wants to be the Agent of Change. When He does the changing, it is permanent. We no longer have to cover sin with fig leaves. He wants us to come to Him. He will make the crooked path straight. The Father has always wanted relationship with His children. If we make a mistake, He always wants to seek us. Don't allow failures to keep you from Him. When Adam and Eve messed up, they covered themselves with fig leaves, trusting in their own merits. Let's trust God.

# Verses To Help You Every Day!

## Strength

"I can do all things through him who strengthens me." (Philippians 4:13)

"Fear not, for I am with you; be not dismayed, for I am your God; I will strengthen you, I will help you, I will uphold you with my righteous right hand."
(Isaiah 41:10)

"Be strong and courageous. Do not fear or be in dread of them, for it is the Lord your God who goes with you. He will not leave you or forsake you." (Deuteronomy 31:6)

"But they who wait for the Lord shall renew their strength; they shall mount up with wings like eagles; they shall run and not be weary; they shall walk and not faint."
(Isaiah 40:31)

"No temptation has overtaken you that is not common to man. God is faithful, and he will not let you be tempted beyond your ability, but with the temptation he will also provide the way of escape, that you may be able to endure it." (1 Corinthians 10:13)

"The Lord is my strength and my song, and he has become my salvation; this is my God, and I will praise him, my father's God, and I will exalt him."
(Exodus 15:2)

"Finally, be strong in the Lord and in the strength of his might." (Ephesians 6:10)

"For the Lord your God is he who goes with you to fight for you against your enemies, to give you the victory." (Deuteronomy 20:4)

"But he said to me, "My grace is sufficient for you, for my power is made perfect in weakness." Therefore I will boast all the more gladly of my weaknesses, so that the power of Christ may rest upon me. For the sake of Christ, then, I am content with weaknesses, insults, hardships, persecutions, and calamities. For when I am weak, then I am strong."
(2 Corinthians 12:9-10)

"Have I not commanded you? Be strong and courageous. Do not be frightened, and do not be dismayed, for the Lord your God is with you wherever you go." (Joshua 1:9)

"For God gave us a spirit not of fear but of power and love and self-control." (2 Timothy 1:7)

"Behold, God is my salvation; I will trust, and will not be afraid; for the Lord God is my strength and my song, and he has become my salvation."
(Isaiah 12:2)

"He gives power to the faint, and to him who has no might he increases strength." (Isaiah 40:29)

"The Lord is my light and my salvation; whom shall I fear? The Lord is the stronghold of my life; of whom shall I be afraid?" (Psalm 27:1)

"Be strong, and let your heart take courage, all you who wait for the Lord!" (Psalm 31:24)

"My flesh and my heart may fail, but God is the strength of my heart and my portion forever."
(Psalm 73:26)

"But he said to me, "My grace is sufficient for you, for my

power is made perfect in weakness." Therefore I will boast all the more gladly of my weaknesses, so that the power of Christ may rest upon me." (2 Corinthians 12:9)

"And you shall love the Lord your God with all your heart and with all your soul and with all your mind and with all your strength." (Mark 12:30)

"God is our refuge and strength, a very present help in trouble." (Psalm 46:1)

"May the Lord give strength to his people! May the Lord bless his people with peace." (Psalm 29:11)

"I have said these things to you, that in me you may have peace. In the world you will have tribulation. But take heart; I have overcome the world." (John 16:33)

"But seek first the kingdom of God and his righteousness, and all these things will be added to you." (Matthew 6:33)

"Even though I walk through the valley of the shadow of death, I will fear no evil, for you are with me; your rod and your staff, they comfort me." (Psalm 23:4)

"The Lord is my strength and my song; he has become my salvation." (Psalm 118:14)

# Verses To Help You Every Day!

## Faith

Faith is what gives us the courage to keep going when we feel overwhelmed. It is through faith in God that we can trust in His goodness. These Scripture quotes teach us the power of God that is available to us when we have faith!

"For nothing will be impossible with God." (Luke 1:37)

"For by grace you have been saved through faith. And this is not your own doing; it is the gift of God, not a result of works, so that no one may boast." (Ephesians 2:8-9)

"Trust in the Lord with all your heart, and do not lean on your own understanding. In all your ways acknowledge him, and he will make straight your paths."
(Proverbs 3:5-6)

"For we walk by faith, not by sight." (2 Corinthians 5:7)

"And Jesus answered them, 'Truly, I say to you, if you have faith and do not doubt, you will not only do what has been done to the fig tree, but even if you say to this mountain, 'Be taken up and thrown into the sea,' it will happen. And whatever you ask in prayer, you will receive, if you have faith." (Matthew 21:21-22)

"And without faith it is impossible to please him, for whoever would draw near to God must believe that he exists and that he rewards those who seek him." (Hebrews 11:6)

"Now faith is the assurance of things hoped for, the conviction of things not seen." (Hebrews 11:1)

"And Jesus answered them, "Have faith in God. Truly, I say to you, whoever says to this mountain, 'Be taken up and thrown into the sea,' and does not doubt in his heart, but believes that what he says will come to pass, it will be done for him. Therefore I tell you, whatever you ask in prayer, believe that you have received it, and it will be yours." (Mark 11:22-24)

"Though you have not seen him, you love him. Though you do not now see him, you believe in him and rejoice with joy that is inexpressible and filled with glory, obtaining the outcome of your faith, the salvation of your souls."
(1 Peter 1:8-9)

"May you be strengthened with all power, according to his glorious might, for all endurance and patience with joy," (Colossians 1:11)

"But let all who take refuge in you rejoice; let them ever sing for joy, and spread your protection over them, that those who love your name may exult in you." (Psalm 5:11)

"You have turned for me my mourning into dancing; you have loosed my sackcloth and clothed me with gladness," (Psalm 30:11)

"Splendor and majesty are before him; strength and joy are in his place." (1 Chronicles 16:27)

# Verses To Help You Every Day!

# Dealing with Fear

God does not want us to fear anything in life because He already won the victory over evil and death. While we may momentarily feel anxieties rise, we can be reminded by these Bible verses that we can trade our worries for joy.

"Peace I leave with you; my peace I give to you. Not as the world gives do I give to you. Let not your hearts be troubled, neither let them be afraid." (John 14:27)

"The LORD is my light and my salvation—whom shall I fear? The LORD is the stronghold of my life—of whom shall I be afraid?" (Psalm 27:1)

"Therefore do not worry about tomorrow, for tomorrow will worry about itself. Each day has enough trouble of its own." (Matthew 6:34)

"Rejoice in hope, be patient in tribulation, be constant in prayer." (Romans 12:12)

"But now, this is what the LORD says—he who created you, Jacob, he who formed you, Israel: "Do not fear, for I have redeemed you; I have summoned you by name; you are mine." (Isaiah 43:1)

"I sought the LORD, and he answered me; he delivered me from all my fears." (Psalm 34:4)

"When anxiety was great within me, your consolation brought me joy." (Psalm 94:19)

"Rejoice in the Lord always; again I will say, Rejoice." (Philippians 4:4)

"But the fruit of the Spirit is love, joy, peace, patience, kindness, goodness, faithfulness," (Galatians 5:22)

"Until now you have asked nothing in my name. Ask, and you will receive, that your joy may be full." (John 16:24)

"A joyful heart is good medicine, but a crushed spirit dries up the bones." (Proverbs 17:22)

"Though you have not seen him, you love him. Though you do not now see him, you believe in him and rejoice with joy that is inexpressible and filled with glory," (1 Peter 1:8)

"So also you have sorrow now, but I will see you again, and your hearts will rejoice, and no one will take your joy from you." (John 16:22)

"This is the day that the Lord has made; let us rejoice and be glad in it." (Psalm 118:24)

"You make known to me the path of life; in your presence there is fullness of joy; at your right hand are pleasures forevermore." (Psalm 16:11)

"These things I have spoken to you, that my joy may be in you, and that your joy may be full." (John 15:11)

"For his anger is but for a moment, and his favor is for a lifetime. Weeping may tarry for the night, but joy comes with the morning." (Psalm 30:5)

"Rejoice always, pray without ceasing, give thanks in all circumstances; for this is the will of God in Christ Jesus for you." (1 Thessalonians 5:16-18)

"Heal me, O Lord, and I will be healed; save me and I will be saved, for you are the one I praise."
(Jeremiah 17:14)

"Is anyone among you sick? Let them call the elders of the church to pray over them and anoint them with oil in the name of the Lord. And the prayer offered in faith will make the sick person well; the Lord will raise them up." (James 5:14-15)

He said, "If you listen carefully to the LORD your God and do what is right in his eyes, if you pay attention to his commands and keep all his decrees, I will not bring on you any of the diseases I brought on the Egyptians, for I am the LORD, who heals you." (Exodus 15:26)

"Worship the LORD your God, and his blessing will be on your food and water. I will take away sickness from among you…" (Exodus 23:25)

"…I am with you; do not be dismayed, for I am your God. I will strengthen you and help you; I will uphold you with my righteous right hand." (Isaiah 41:10)

# Verses To Help You Every Day!

## Healing

"Surely he took up our pain and bore our suffering, yet we considered him punished by God, stricken by him, and afflicted. But he was pierced for our transgressions, he was crushed for our iniquities; the punishment that brought us peace was on him, and by his wounds we are healed." (Isaiah 53:4-5)

"But I will restore you to health and heal your wounds,' declares the LORD" (Jeremiah 30:17)

"See now that I myself am he! There is no god besides me. I put to death and I bring to life, I have wounded and I will heal, and no one can deliver out of my hand." (Deuteronomy 32:39)

"If my people, who are called by my name, will humble themselves and pray and seek my face and turn from their wicked ways, then I will hear from heaven, and I will forgive their sin and will heal their land. Now my eyes will be open and my ears attentive to the prayers offered in this place." (2 Chronicles 7:14-15)

"You restored me to health and let me live. Surely it was for my benefit that I suffered such anguish. In your love you kept me from the pit of destruction; you have put all my sins behind your back." (Isaiah 38:16-17)

"I have seen their ways, but I will heal them; I will guide them and restore comfort to Israel's mourners, creating praise on their lips. Peace, peace, to those far and near," says the LORD. "And I will heal them." (Isaiah 57:18-19)

"Nevertheless, I will bring health and healing to it; I will heal my people and will let them enjoy abundant peace and security." (Jeremiah 33:6)

"Dear friend, I pray that you may enjoy good health and that all may go well with you, even as your soul is getting along well." (3 John 1:2)

"He will wipe every tear from their eyes. There will be no more death or mourning or crying or pain, for the old order of things has passed away." (Revelations 21:4)

# Verses To Help You Every Day!

# Praise and Worship

"The LORD is my strength and song, and he is become my salvation: he is my God, and I will prepare him an habitation; my father's God, and I will exalt him." (Exodus 15:2)

"Because I will publish the name of the LORD: ascribe ye greatness unto our God." (Deuteronomy 32:3)

"Therefore I will give thanks unto thee, O LORD, among the heathen, and I will sing praises unto thy name." (2 Samuel 22:50)

"Give thanks unto the LORD, call upon his name, make known his deeds among the people. Sing unto him, sing psalms unto him, talk ye of all his wondrous works. Glory ye in his holy name: let the heart of them rejoice that seek the LORD." (1 Chronicles 16:8-10)

"Blessed be the God and Father of our Lord Jesus Christ, which according to his abundant mercy hath begotten us again unto a lively hope by the resurrection of Jesus Christ from the dead," (1 Peter 1:3)

"And every creature which is in heaven, and on the earth, and under the earth, and such as are in the sea, and all that are in them, heard I saying, Blessing, and honour, and glory, and power, be unto him that sitteth upon the throne, and unto the Lamb for ever and ever." (Revelation 5:13)

"Now therefore, our God, we thank thee, and praise thy glorious name." (1 Chronicles 29:13)

"I will bless the LORD, who hath given me counsel: my reins also instruct me in the night seasons." (Psalm 16:7)

"Sing praises to the LORD, which dwelleth in Zion: declare among the people his doings." (Psalm 9:11)

"And immediately he received his sight, and followed him, glorifying God: and all the people, when they saw it, gave praise unto God." (Luke 18:43)

"Rejoice in the Lord alway: and again I say, Rejoice." (Philippians 4:4)

"O sing unto the LORD a new song: sing unto the LORD,

all the earth. Sing unto the LORD, bless his name; shew forth his salvation from day to day." (Psalm 96:1-2)

"Bless ye the LORD, all ye his hosts; ye ministers of his, that do his pleasure." (Psalm 103:21)

"O praise the LORD, all ye nations: praise him, all ye people. For his merciful kindness is great toward us: and the truth of the LORD endureth for ever. Praise ye the LORD." (Psalm 117:1-2)

"Bless ye the LORD, all ye his hosts; ye ministers of his, that do his pleasure." (Psalm 103:21)

"And immediately he received his sight, and followed him, glorifying God: and all the people, when they saw it, gave praise unto God." (Luke 18:43)

"Now unto the King eternal, immortal, invisible, the only wise God, be honour and glory for ever and ever. Amen." (1 Timothy 1:17)

Endnotes

1	https://www.tcpi.com/psychological-impact-light-color/

2	https://www.urbandictionary.com/define.php?term=Microwave%20Society

www.ingramcontent.com/pod-product-compliance
Lightning Source LLC
Chambersburg PA
CBHW052109110526
44592CB00013B/1543